Alexander invades Egypt. He frees the Egyptian people from Persian rule and is made Pharaoh. He builds a new city in Egypt and names it Alexandria.

Alexander's army storms the Persian cities of Babylon and Persepolis.

Alexander invades India and is victorious in a battle with a local leader, King Porus. Alexander now calls himself "Lord of all Asia". Bucephalus, Alexander's horse, dies from battle wounds.

Alexander dies at Babylon, the centre of his empire. He is just 32 years old.

| 333 BC | 332 BC | 331 BC | 330 BC | 327 BC | 326 BC | 324 BC | 323 BC |

Alexander and King Darius III of Persia meet at the Battle of Issus. Alexander's army is victorious, but Darius escapes.

Alexander and King Darius III of Persia meet again at Gaugamela. Alexander's army wins the battle. Once again Darius escapes but is eventually murdered by his own men.

Around this time Alexander marries one of his captives, a princess called Roxane.

Alexander marries his second wife, King Darius's daughter Statira, in a mass wedding ceremony at Susa. Over 90 of Alexander's men marry Persian women.

First published in Great Britain in 2003 by Brimax
An imprint of Octopus Publishing Group Ltd
2-4 Heron Quays, London E14 4JP

A CIP catalogue record for this book is available from the British Library.

ISBN 1 85854 481 5 (hardback)
ISBN 185854 707 5 (paperback)

Created by *ticktock* Media Ltd.

Printed in China

# ALEXANDER
## THE GREAT

By Penny Worms

Illustrated by Anthony Lewis

## CONTENTS

BRIMAX

# Birth of a Royal Baby

In the summer of 356 BC, a baby boy was born to King **Philip II** of **Macedon**, and his main wife, Queen **Olympias**. The king and queen and their son, Alexander, lived in a white palace, high on a hill overlooking the capital city of Macedon, **Pella**. Macedon was a beautiful, mountainous kingdom situated in the north of **Greece**. Even though Alexander was looked after by the palace slaves, the young prince was still very close to his mother and lived with her in the women's quarters of the palace. As a baby, Alexander was wrapped in expensive cotton from **India**, and silks from the East. As a boy he had toy soldiers to play with, and he learned to read, write, and play music.

## A WOMAN'S WORK

The main work for ancient Greek women was to ensure that their households ran smoothly. Wealthy women simply had to give orders to their slaves, but poor women had to do all the jobs around the home themselves, and work on the family farm. All Greek girls, rich or poor, were taught how to spin wool and weave cloth. Even Alexander's sisters, the royal princesses, would spend their days weaving and spinning!

## Life as a Slave

I must be the busiest slave in the whole kingdom of Macedon! I have been chosen to take care of the new prince, Alexander. The palace is huge with many rooms - it is so different to my family's one-room home in the city. Baby Alexander is very sweet but a bit of a handful. I prepare his meals and keep him clean and tidy, which is quite a big job! He slides on the stone floors and hides behind tall columns and statues. Now that he can crawl I need eyes in the back of my head; he nearly tumbled into one of the wells in the courtyard yesterday. What a determined little boy!

Children from ordinary families had a much tougher start in life. They had little or no education, and no slaves to help at home. Boys were expected to help their father on the farm and girls helped their mother with the household chores. Families in the countryside had small areas of land, on which they grew much of the food that they needed. Growing crops was hard work as the soil was rocky and poor, and the weather dry and hot. Some lucky farmers owned their own oxen to pull the plough, but many communities had to share. Really poor farmers would only have a mule.

# King Philip's Kingdom

When Alexander was growing up, Greece was not a single, united country, as it is today. All the people spoke the same language and worshipped the same gods, but the region was divided into separate **city-states**, each ruled by the **citizens** themselves. Every male citizen aged eighteen and over was able to vote in elections, but women, children, and slaves did not have this right. Regular meetings were held to allow the citizens to make important decisions and pass laws. This made each city-state a **democracy** and this way of government made the city-states feel superior to kingdoms like Macedon, who still had kings ruling over them. When King Philip came to the throne in 359 BC, Macedon was a poor land and his people were considered barbarians, but Philip had great plans. He conquered **Amphipolis**, a city that had many gold mines and used the gold to train soldiers and buy them weapons. He then attacked and conquered Macedon's neighbouring regions of **Thessaly** and **Thrace**. Macedon was becoming rich and strong and Philip was creating an empire.

Alexander learned a lot from his father. He saw how successful Philip was with a large, well-trained army and good battle plans. Philip even developed a new way for his infantry soldiers to march on their enemies called the **Macedonian Phalanx**. Throughout this time the Greek city-states of **Athens**, **Thebes**, and **Sparta** had been fighting amongst themselves and had not noticed how strong Macedon had become. Philip now turned his attention to the city-states. His ambition was to conquer them all and unite the whole of Greece.

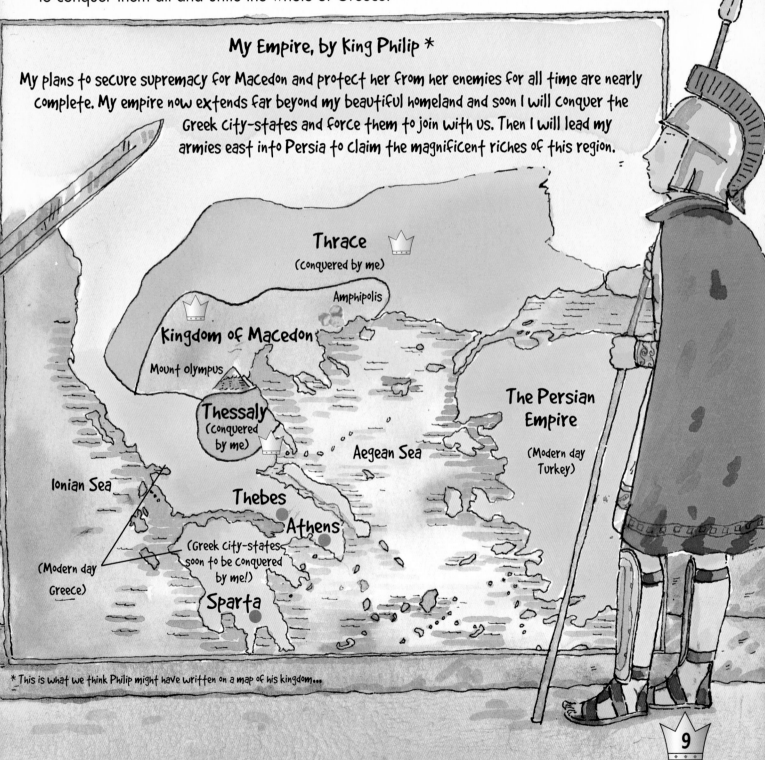

### My Empire, by King Philip *

My plans to secure supremacy for Macedon and protect her from her enemies for all time are nearly complete. My empire now extends far beyond my beautiful homeland and soon I will conquer the Greek city-states and force them to join with us. Then I will lead my armies east into Persia to claim the magnificent riches of this region.

Thrace
(Conquered by me)

Amphipolis

Kingdom of Macedon

Mount Olympus

Thessaly
(Conquered by me)

Ionian Sea

Thebes

Athens

(Greek city-states soon to be conquered by me!)

(Modern day Greece)

Sparta

Aegean Sea

The Persian Empire

(Modern day Turkey)

* This is what we think Philip might have written on a map of his kingdom...

# Alexander and Bucephalus

When Alexander was about 12 years old, a horse dealer brought Philip a magnificent, wild stallion. Philip asked the best horsemen in his kingdom to ride the horse to see if he should buy it. One by one, riders from across the land tried to mount the horse but he was uncontrollable and would not be ridden. Alexander boasted that he would be able to ride the horse and asked his father if he could try. Alexander had noticed that the horse was frightened by the movements of its own shadow. Philip issued a challenge to his son – if Alexander could ride the horse, he could have him!

### CHARIOT RACING

Chariot racing was a sport in ancient Greece. Chariots were usually pulled around a race-track by two or four horses. It was a hugely popular form of entertainment, but was dangerous for both horses and charioteers.

## My Best Friend
## by Alexander *

Hephaistion is my best friend in the whole world! He is the son of one of my father's companions and so we get to spend a lot of time together. We even study together (although our tutors probably wish they could split us up!) Hephaistion is good-looking and clever, but he is not as good at hunting and riding as me. We get on so well that I think the two of us will be friends forever.

\* This is what we think Alexander might have said about his best friend!

Alexander walked up to the horse and spoke softly to him. He gently turned the horse around so he was facing the sun and could not see his shadow. To everyone's amazement, Alexander mounted the horse and rode off into the sun. Philip was so impressed that he bought the horse for Alexander, who named him **Bucephalus** (meaning 'ox head', because of the shape of his skull). No one else ever rode Bucephalus and he was always Alexander's favourite horse. They rode thousands of miles and fought many battles together. When Bucephalus died of battle wounds, Alexander held a big funeral for the horse, and named a city after him.

# Schooldays with Aristotle

When Alexander was about thirteen, his father, Philip, brought the greatest thinker of the day, the **philosopher Aristotle**, to Macedon. Aristotle was Alexander's teacher for three years and taught him about politics and literature. Other boys went to schools. They started at the age of seven and were taken to and from school by a slave called a **pedagogue**, who stayed with the boys and beat them if they didn't work hard. Girls didn't go to school, but some were taught at home.

## ANCIENT CALCULATORS

The ancient Greeks did their sums on an **abacus** – one of the earliest kinds of calculator. Rows of beads represent numbers. One row is the ones, another is the tens, another is the hundreds, and so on.

Children practised writing by using a pointed stick called a stylus to scratch letters into the soft wax-coated surface of a writing tablet.

## My Tutor Aristotle, by Alexander *

Aristotle is a great tutor, but his lessons are really tiring and he never stops walking up and down! Still, he is a real mastermind, dedicated to trying to make sense of our world through study, thought, questioning, and argument. He has inspired my love for the writings of our great Greek playwrights and poets. He has even given me his copy of the "Iliad", the poet Homer's thrilling account of the Trojan wars. I've already read it loads of times, and I carry it with me everywhere!

* Alexander might have written something like this at school.

Boys spent the first few years at school learning to read, write, and count. They had music lessons, too, and learned to play the flute (**aulos**) and the lyre (**kithara**). When they were in their teens, boys took part in athletics and were taught to wrestle and box. Before they left school at eighteen, they also studied the art of public speaking.

### GREEK ALPHABET

This is the classical Greek alphabet that Alexander would have studied. The word alphabet comes from the first two letters, alpha and beta. It formed the basis of the 26-letter Roman alphabet this book is written in.

| | |
|---|---|
| Α | **Alpha** |
| Β | **Beta** |
| Γ | **Gamma** |
| Δ | **Delta** |
| Ε | **Epsilon** |
| Ζ | **Zeta** |
| Η | **Eta** |
| Θ | **Theta** |
| Ι | **Iota** |
| Κ | **Kappa** |
| Λ | **Lambda** |
| Μ | **Mu** |
| Ν | **Nu** |
| Ξ | **Xi** |
| Ο | **Omicron** |
| Π | **Pi** |
| Ρ | **Rho** |
| Σ | **Sigma** |
| Τ | **Tau** |
| Υ | **Upsilon** |
| Φ | **Phi** |
| Χ | **Chi** |
| Ψ | **Psi** |
| Ω | **Omega** |

# The Olympic Games

Every four years, a spectacular sporting event took place in Greece, at **Olympia**. It was called the **Olympic Games** and the finest athletes from all the city-states met to honour the gods by competing against one another. Their aim was to see who could run the fastest, throw the furthest, and beat the very best from other city-states. A winning athlete received a crown of olive leaves cut from a sacred tree. But more important than this prize was the chance for an athlete to take glory back to his city-state. Winning athletes were treated like heroes on their return home.

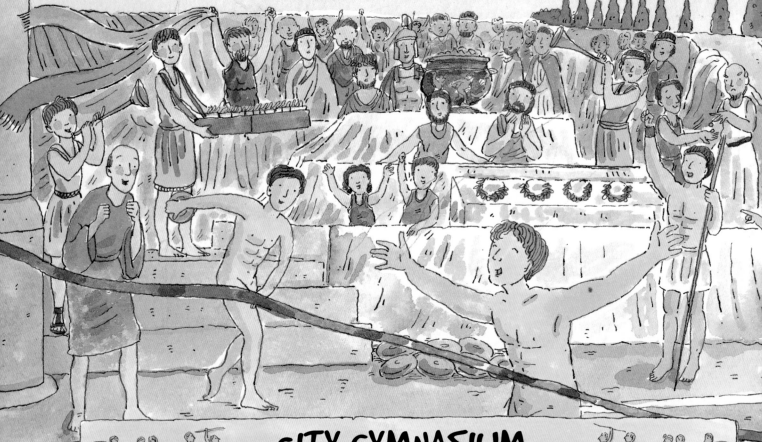

## CITY GYMNASIUM

### • STAY HEALTHY • PLEASE THE GODS
### • IDEAL TRAINING FOR SOLDIERS • ALL THE LATEST EQUIPMENT

Running track (no rocks or chariot ruts)
Javelins (new lightweight designs)
Discus (stone and bronze available)

Slaves (for boxing and wrestling practice)
Chariots (horses provided – one piece of gold to be given as a deposit)

• **Open daily sunrise to sunset** • **Free wine and bread for all members**

Even wars between the city-states were stopped or postponed so that the Olympic games could take place, and competitors and spectators could travel safely to the event. On the opening day, all the athletes went to the temple of **Zeus** (the king of the gods) where they swore to abide by the rules. Then the games began. Thousands of men from all over the Greek world flocked to the games to watch competitors throw the javelin and discus, race horses and chariots, box and wrestle. All the athletes competed in the nude, except for the **hoplite** soldiers who had to run in full armour! Women and slaves were not allowed to attend and this particularly angered the girls of Sparta, who were excellent athletes. However, they risked being thrown off a cliff if they disobeyed the rules of the Olympic games.

## Olympic Champions by Alexander *

Soon it will be time for the Olympic games to be held again. I'm hoping that the Macedonian athletes will win lots of the events. When I am older, I plan to compete in the games. My horse riding skills are now so good that I am sure I will win an olive crown and bring back glory to Macedon! The Games last for five days:

DAY 1 – Running events
DAY 2 – Pentathlon (five events of running, wrestling, long jump, javelin, and discus)
DAY 3 – Horse racing
DAY 4 – Chariot racing
DAY 5 – Boxing and wrestling

I know that to compete and honour the gods I must be fit and healthy, so I will train hard every day and continue to practise my riding skills.

* We think Alexander might have thought this!

# Food and Drink

As Alexander got older, he spent more time with his father, whenever Philip was home from war. The king loved to hold parties in the palace. Only important male guests were invited, and the eating and drinking would take place in a special men-only dining room. The guests would be treated to plates of wild boar and deer, fried squid, cheese, olives, salads, and bread. Bread was eaten daily by most Greeks, whether rich or poor. It was made from wheat or barley flour, and was coarse and stodgy.

## King Philip's Feast *

Octopus tentacles sliced and boiled in olive oil.
Macedonian goat's cheese.
Wild boar with garlic and onion.
Rabbit cooked with turnips and beans,
sprinkled with fresh herbs from the mountains.
Locally caught tuna fish.

### SIDE ORDERS
Hard-boiled eggs.
Fresh local peas.
Olive oil with bread for dipping.
Sweetmeats of finest sesame seeds rolled in honey.
Melon and pomegranate surprise.
Wine grown in the king's vineyard
and trodden by the cleanest
feet in the region.

* This is what the menu at Philip's banquet might have looked like!

### WINE

Wine was a favourite drink in Greece, whether you were rich or poor, but the drinking vessels were different. Glass was very expensive so only the wealthy could afford to drink from glass goblets. Ordinary people had goblets made from clay baked hard in an oven.

### OLIVES AND OLIVE OIL

The goddess **Athena** is said to have brought olive trees to Greece. The olives were either eaten or pressed to make oil for cooking and for pouring on salads. The oil could also be burned to create lighting in houses and was even used as a beauty product, rubbed into the skin to make it smoother and softer.

At every one of Philip's parties, the wine flowed freely. All Greek wine was so thick it had to be strained before drinking. Other Greeks mixed their wine with water, but the Macedonians preferred theirs undiluted – getting extremely drunk was a common occurrence at a Macedonian party! To complete the feast, the guests were offered delicious sweetmeats made from dates, figs, nuts, and honey, while being entertained by acrobats and musicians. After the meal the men would stay to drink even more wine and have important discussions. These after-dinner talking and drinking sessions were known as **symposiums**.

# Dressing Up for the Theatre

Greek men loved going to the theatre, and Alexander would have attended regularly with his father, sitting in the front row on the best seats. There were open-air theatres in most cities in Greece and even the poor could afford this popular form of entertainment. The tickets were inexpensive and sometimes free as wealthy patrons and politicians would pay for the actors to put on a play. When the play started, the **chorus** would enter the circle in front of the stage. As the chorus told the story, the actors would perform behind them on the stage. The actors wore masks and would change their mask to become a different character, or to change their mood from happy to sad.

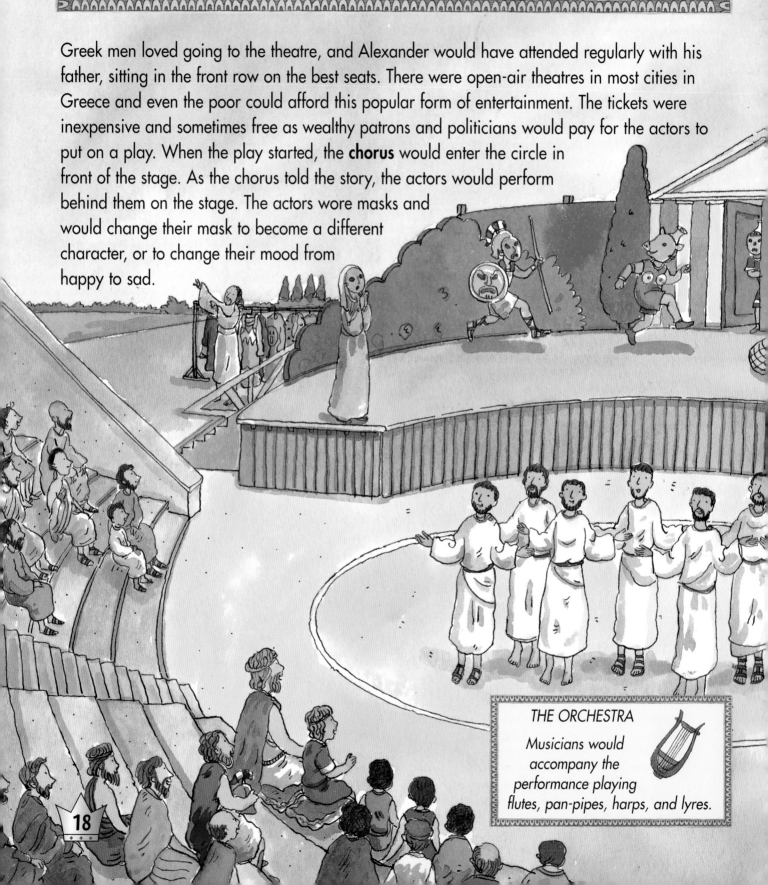

THE ORCHESTRA

Musicians would accompany the performance playing flutes, pan-pipes, harps, and lyres.

# TODAY AT
# THE PELLA THEATRE

**MEDEA** by Euripides (a tragedy)

**AGAMEMNON** by Aeschylus

**THE CLOUDS**
by Aristophanes (a new comedy)

**OEDIPUS THE KING** by Sophocles

Greek actors were always male. The
younger boys would play the female parts,
wearing wigs. The actors would speak
their parts and sometimes sing them. The
plays were usually comedies or tragedies:
the most popular by far were the tragedies,
the gloomier the better! A visit to the theatre was
a good opportunity for rich Greek families to dress up in their
finest clothes and show off their wealth. Even poor people
would wear their best tunics, although they would probably be
made of finely spun wool, not silk or cotton.

## ANCIENT GREEK FASHION

The ancient Greeks paid
a great deal of attention
to their clothing and
hairstyles. Both men and
women wore white or
brightly coloured tunics
fastened at the shoulder
with a brooch. Rich people
wore gold and silver
necklaces and earrings,
while the poor wore
jewellery made of bronze.
Hair was curled into the
latest styles and make-up
was used by both men
and women to cover
unfashionable suntans.

# Alexander – Regent and King

At sixteen, Alexander was left in charge of Macedon as **regent**, while Philip went away to war. Everyone admired Alexander's intelligence, hunting skills, and horsemanship, and he quickly proved himself as a leader and **general**. On receiving word that there was a barbarian rebellion east of Macedon, Alexander led an army to the barbarians' largest city and crushed the rebels. Philip was so impressed with his son that, two years later, he put Alexander in command of the **cavalry** in the **Battle of Chaeronea**. Alexander's bravery in leading his men straight into the enemy ranks helped Philip to win this decisive battle against Athens and her allies. Philip was now the ruler of most of Greece, but just as he reached the height of his power he was murdered. Alexander was just twenty years old.

## My Army, by Alexander *

I have gathered together the very best fighters from all over Greece.

*30,000 foot soldiers from Macedon, Greece, and the Balkans.
*5,000 cavalry from Macedon and Thessaly.
*Archers from Crete.
*Scouts from Thrace to keep watch for the enemy.
*Artists, poets, and writers to record my achievements.
*Builders to lay out our camps.
*Grooms to care for the horses and mules.
*My servants.

Hephaistion and Bucephalus are with me.
How can I lose? I will soon be the leader of a huge empire, where there is peace and equality for all.

* This is what we think Alexander might have written about his army!

To become the new king of Macedon, Alexander had to be accepted by the army. This proved no problem as they already loved him. He was hailed king on the day of his father's death. He said, "Nothing has changed except the name of the king!" However, some Greek states rebelled against being ruled by a young Macedonian king. But Alexander was ruthless. He crushed every rebellion to finally unite Greece. And, when his father's most recent new wife and her baby were murdered, it was believed that Alexander had been involved. No one would come between Alexander and the throne of Macedon.

### MACEDONIAN PHALANX

Philip's success in battle was partly due to how he trained his foot soldiers. Marching in rows, the rear troops held their 6 m. (19.5 ft.) long pikes upright while the front soldiers held theirs out in front of them. In this way, they could easily spear the enemy, but from a safe distance!

# Oracles and the Gods

Many different gods and goddesses were worshipped in ancient Greece. If you needed to ask a god for help or to thank them for something good in your life, the best way to do this was to visit their temple and pay for an animal to be sacrificed. If Alexander needed their help to make a really important decision or to solve a problem he would consult an **oracle**. At the oracle the visitor paid to ask the gods a question. Surrounded by burning incense, and in a deep trance, the high priestess or **Pythia** would communicate directly with the gods. The Pythia's answer to your question was normally complete gibberish but interpreters were on hand to explain the meaning of the message. Alexander visited the oracle at the temple of **Apollo**, in **Delphi**, before he invaded **Persia**.

*ATHENA*

*Each of the gods in ancient Greece had their own roles and were worshipped in their own temples. The temple called the **Parthenon** in Athens was built for the goddess Athena, daughter of the king of the gods, Zeus. Athena was the goddess of wisdom and warfare and also the patron goddess of Athens, which was named in her honour.*

## Meet the Ancient Greek Gods

ARTEMIS was the goddess of the moon, hunting, and small children. She used silver arrows and could out-shoot any mortal.

POSEIDON was the god of the sea and of earthquakes. He didn't live on Mount Olympus but under the ocean in an underwater palace, where he watched over sailors and sea creatures.

 APHRODITE was the goddess of love, desire, and beauty. She could make any man or god fall in love with her.

HEPHAESTUS was the god of craftsmen and blacksmiths. He made weapons for the gods.

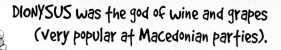

APOLLO was the god of sunlight, crops, and music.

DIONYSUS was the god of wine and grapes (very popular at Macedonian parties).

The ancient Greeks believed that their twelve most important gods lived on **Mount Olympus,** in the north of the country. Zeus was the king of the gods and god of the Heavens. When people heard thunder they believed that Zeus was angry at something on Earth. He was all-powerful and a master of disguise, often coming down to earth in the form of a bull or a swan. His queen was **Hera**, the goddess of women and marriage. The gods behaved just like people on Earth – they fought and fell in love, and would often meddle in the lives of mortal people.

# Alexander's Campaigns

Now that Greece was united, Alexander turned his attention to the Persian Empire to the East, ruled by King **Darius III**. Persia had successfully invaded Greece in the past, but now it was time for the Greeks to strike back. Alexander marched east, winning battle after battle. Finally, in 333 BC he came face to face with King Darius III on the battlefield at **Issus**. Alexander's tactics and bravery won the day with the loss of only a few hundred men. But Darius escaped. Two years later they met again and this time Darius had even more men, with horses, chariots, and elephants. Darius and his generals were so confident of victory, they had brought their families along to watch. Darius even chose the battleground, at **Gaugamela** (in modern day Iraq).

## My Battle Diary, by Alexander *

*334 BC - Left Greece to invade Persia.

*333 BC - First battle with King Darius III at Issus - we won but tricky Darius escaped.

*332 BC - We freed Egypt from Persian rule. I was made Pharaoh and built a magnificent city in Egypt. I called it Alexandria in my honour.

*331 BC - King Darius III and I met again on the battlefield at Gaugamela. We won again.

*330 BC - We stormed the Persian cities of Babylon and Persepolis. We found enough silver and gold to pay the soldiers' wages for many years.

*326 BC - We fought King Porus in India. My dear Bucephalus died. I built a city on the site of the battlefield and named it after him.

* As Alexander might have recorded his battles.

The Persians were to be disappointed yet again. Alexander's superior leadership led the Greek army to victory. Once again Darius escaped, but the Persians had lost faith in their king and he was eventually murdered by his own men. Alexander was now leader of the whole Persian Empire. In 326 BC, Alexander marched further east and invaded the strange and unknown land of India. This time the Greek army faced an entirely new and terrifying foe – the specially trained war elephants of King **Porus**, who ruled part of India. Although Porus's army was very strong with more than 100 elephants, the brilliant young general was once again victorious. Alexander now called himself "Lord of all Asia".

# Alexander's Marriages

Alexander continued to push east, capturing more land and people. He had fallen in love with one of his captives – a princess called **Roxane** from **Bactria**, an area to the north east of the Persian empire and they had married. Alexander pressed on into India and conquered many cities, until his men reached breaking point. They had invaded India during the rainy season and Alexander's soldiers were tired of marching through floodwaters, full of dangerous snakes and crocodiles. They had been away from Greece for almost ten years and they wanted to go home. Alexander reluctantly agreed, and the Greek army headed back to Persia. When Alexander returned to the city of **Susa** there was unrest among the Persian people. To promote harmony between East and West, he held a mass marriage ceremony.

### Roxane *
### (Alexander's first wife)

My real name is Roshanak, meaning little star. Alexander thinks me very beautiful and he fell in love with me as soon as he saw me. I was just sixteen when we were married and I was delighted to soon fall pregnant. Sadly I lost our baby. I bravely followed Alexander to India.

### Statira *
### (Alexander's second wife)

I was originally named Barsine, but I took my mother's name of Statira when she died. I was about fifteen when I married Alexander, and needed to find a husband because I have no father to support me and cannot earn a living for myself. Although Alexander is responsible for my father's death I trust him to be a strong and brave husband to me.

* This is how Alexander's wives might have introduced themselves.

Alexander took a second wife, **Statira**, who was King Darius's daughter. Hephaistion married Statira's sister and ninety other high-ranking men in Alexander's army were ordered to marry Persia's finest ladies. At the mass wedding ceremony all the bridegrooms sat in seats arranged in rows. After a banquet the brides came in and sat next to their husbands. Each bridegroom then took hold of his bride's right hand and kissed it. Alexander was the first to begin, with his men then following his lead. Over the course of time, 10,000 Macedonian soldiers married Persian woman and even Alexander took a third wife, **Parysatis**, the daughter of another Persian king.

# Death of Alexander

In 323 BC, Alexander went back to Babylon, now the centre of his empire. He started to make plans to conquer more lands in Arabia and North Africa. His best friend, Hephaistion, had died the year before and the summer was hot and humid. Alexander suddenly fell ill with a fever, possibly malaria. His generals were waiting for the orders to put his new plans into action but when they heard nothing, they knew something was wrong. Realising that Alexander was close to death, his generals asked him who was to inherit his empire. Alexander just said, "Whoever is the strongest". A few days later he died, at the age of 32.

## THE NEW KING

*Alexander's first wife, Roxane, was pregnant when Alexander died. She had a son who became King **Alexander IV**. The young boy shared his crown for a while with Alexander's half brother, but he was murdered in the power struggles that followed Alexander's death. The alliances that Alexander had built eventually crumbled and his empire was torn apart.*

## THE LEGACY OF THE ANCIENT GREEKS

The ancient Greeks have influenced many aspects of our lives today.
Ancient art and architecture inspire us, and many modern governments
are based on the Greek idea of democracy. An evening at the theatre is still a popular pastime,
with modern theatres based on the ancient Greek design. And every four years athletes from
across the world compete at the Olympic Games for medals, and glory!

At the time of his death, Alexander's empire extended from Greece to India, a distance of 3,000 miles. Greece was united and Alexander was regarded by the Persians and Egyptians as their leader. His huge army was made up of men from many different races, all prepared to fight under his leadership. The Greek language and currency were used throughout the empire and many new cities had been built and named **Alexandria** in his honour. Even today the Egyptian city of Alexandria is still the second largest in Egypt and the country's main port – just as Alexander had planned. The building of such a vast empire was an extraordinary achievement and the young Macedonian king would be known throughout history as Alexander the Great.

# Glossary

**ABACUS** A calculating machine that uses beads.

**ALEXANDER IV** Alexander the Great's son.

**ALEXANDRIA** An Egyptian city built by Alexander and named in his honour.

**AMPHIPOLIS** A place to the east of Macedonia.

**APHRODITE** The Greek goddess of love, desire, and beauty.

**APOLLO** The Greek god of sunlight, crops, and music.

**ARISTOTLE** The famous philosopher and Alexander's tutor.

**ARTEMIS** The Greek goddess of the moon, hunting, and small children.

**ATHENA** The Greek goddess of wisdom and warfare.

**ATHENS** A Greek city-state, now the capital of Greece.

**AULOS** A type of flute.

**BABYLON** An ancient city in the Persian Empire. Alexander died here.

**BACTRIA** An area in the north east of the Persian Empire.

**BATTLE OF CHAERONEA** A battle between King Philip's army and the Greek city-states (including Athens). This battle finally brought the city-states under Philip's control.

**BUCEPHALUS** Alexander's favourite horse.

**CAVALRY** The part of an army that is made up of soldiers on horseback.

**CHORUS** The narrators of ancient Greek plays.

**CITIZEN** A person who lived in one of the city-states. Citizens were the only people with the right to vote.

**CITY-STATE** The areas that ancient Greece was divided into. Each city-state included a major city and the surrounding countryside.

**DARIUS III** The king of the Persian Empire.

**DELPHI** An ancient Greek city to the north of Athens.

**DEMOCRACY** A system that allows ordinary people to have a say in the running of their country.

**DIONYSUS** The Greek god of wine and grapes.

**GENERAL** A leader of an army.

**GREECE** A southern European country, with coastline on the Mediterranean Sea.

**GAUGAMELA** The name of a village close to the battlefield where Alexander met Darius III in battle, for the second time.

**HEPHAESTUS** The Greek god of craftsmen and blacksmiths.

**HEPHAISTION** Alexander's best friend.

**HERA** The Greek goddess of women and marriage. Wife of Zeus and queen of the gods.

**HOPLITES** Greek foot soldiers who carried swords or spears.

**INDIA** A country in Asia to the east of Greece and the Persian Empire.

**ISSUS** The place in Persia where Alexander and Darius III first met in battle.

**KITHARA** A string instrument similar to a harp.

**MACEDON** A kingdom in the north of Greece.

**MACEDONIAN PHALANX** King Philip's infantry soldiers, who marched in tightly-packed rows with long pikes held out in front of them.

**MOUNT OLYMPUS** A mountain in the north of Greece. The ancient Greeks believed their gods lived here.

**OLYMPIA** A city in the west of Greece.

**OLYMPIAS** King Philip's main wife and mother of Alexander.

**OLYMPIC GAMES** An important sporting event that took place in ancient Greece every four years.

**ORACLE** A special shrine where you could ask the gods questions about your future. A high priestess in a trance would communicate directly with the gods.

**PARTHENON** A temple in Athens built in honour of the goddess Athena.

**PARYSATIS** Alexander's third wife.

**PEDAGOGUE** A slave who accompanied boys to school to ensure that they behaved and worked hard.

**PELA** The capital city of Macedon.

**PERSIA** An ancient empire, stretching from Greece to India.

**PHILIP II** The king of Macedon and father of Alexander.

**PHILOSOPHER** A person who asks questions about how the world works. In ancient Greece, philosophers also studied politics, human behaviour, and science.

**PORUS** An Indian king.

**POSEIDON** The Greek god of the sea and of earthquakes.

**PYTHIA** The high priestess at an oracle.